All About Worries and Fears

A note for grown-ups

This book is about recognizing, understanding and managing anxiety, and it's designed to be shared with young children. At the back of the book, you will find lots more ideas for how to help your children learn to manage their anxieties and become more resilient. There's also advice on how to tell when a young child is overly anxious, and when you should seek professional help.

Contents

Usborne

All About Worries and Fears

Felicity Brooks

Illustrated by Mar Ferrero

Designed by Frankie Allen

With expert advice from
Dr Angharad Rudkin, Clinical Psychologist

What are worries and fears?

Worries are feelings that come from inside our heads that can make us **feel unhappy** or **upset**. All kinds of different things may make us feel worried, but some people worry more than others.

A worry can be quite BIG . . .

or really very small . . .

And EVERYBODY sometimes worries . . .

Grown-ups worry.

Children worry.

Even pets worry.

You can't always tell that someone is worried, and sometimes we don't even know what we are worried about! But worrying is NORMAL (and a little bit of worrying can even be helpful).

A fear is when someone feels **scared** or **afraid** or **frightened**, but not everyone feels afraid of the same things. Here are a few things that some people find a bit scary (but others don't mind, or even like).

Being away from somebody

The dark

Loud noises

Spiders and bugs

Can you think of anything you like that someone else finds scary?

What worries and fears feel like

Even though they're normal, worries and fears DON'T FEEL VERY NICE.
This is what some children say their worries and fears feel like.

"Like a HUGE bag on my back weighing me down."

EURGH, this is so annoying!

ITCH
ITCH
ITCH

"Like an ITCH I can't scratch."

"Like my body has been FROZEN."

STOP!
STOP!

"Like my head is too full."

This is SO hard!

SQUELCH

"Like I'm trying to walk through thick, sticky mud."

WHIRRR SPIN

"Like I have a washing machine inside my tummy."

6

When we are very worried or afraid, our bodies may start to do some things that we can't control. We may find that we...

burst into tears,

start sweating and go red in the face,

I feel wobbly.

begin to shake or tremble,

So do I!

I feel like I can't breathe.

breathe too fast, or get a tummy ache,

have itchy hands,

I feel like I've swallowed a butterfly.

feel our heart beating very fast,

have flappy arms,

I need another wee!

or need the toilet...A LOT!

Do any of these things ever happen to YOU? They are quite normal, and there's lots you can do to help them go away so that you feel calmer. But first it's useful to know WHY our bodies do this...

Why does all this happen?

Our bodies sometimes do things we can't control because they're getting us ready to FACE DANGER. And this can happen even when we're safe because our brains can't tell the difference between a real danger, and something that can't really harm us.

So, our brains send a message to our bodies – a bit like an alarm bell going off.

This makes our hearts beat faster, makes us feel sweaty, speeds up our breathing, makes us wobbly and so on.

This boy is worried because he has a test at school.

And all this happens because a very long time ago there WERE lots of very dangerous things around. So at any moment people needed to be ready to . . .

FIGHT!	FREEZE!	FLEE!

SCREAM and SHOUT to **scare away** a huge bird.

Keep VERY STILL so a bear wouldn't notice them.

RUN AWAY very fast from a poisonous snake.

Nowadays, most of us don't meet dangerous wild animals very often, but our brains still tell our bodies to get ready if they THINK something could be dangerous (even when there's really nothing to be scared of).

But where do our fears come from? Well, they can start in different ways. Here are some.

We may LEARN to be scared of things from other people when we are little.

Some things that make us scared come from our IMAGINATIONS or dreams.

Or from something we've watched or read about and found scary.

Or because something once gave us a nasty surprise or a SHOCK.

A few people have unusual fears of things that really couldn't hurt them.

Do you know anyone who has an unusual fear?

Growing worries and fears

If we don't learn ways to do something about our worries and fears, ones that start quite small can start to GROW. Then they may GROW and GROW until they are ALL we can think about.

They may even get SO BIG, they stop us from feeling happy and stop us from doing things we usually enjoy ...

I really want to go to Arlo's party. All my friends are going and it will be fun ...

BUT ... my dad won't be with me, and there may be BALLOONS ...

And what if I am near the balloons?

And what if one suddenly POPS?

And it SCARES me like it did at that party when I was little?

INVITATION for SAM

BANG!

If you have a worry that starts to grow and grow like this, the GOOD NEWS is that there's lots you can do to stop it and not let it upset you so much. The very first thing to do is sit down and ...

B-r-e-a-t-h-e

When you're worried or scared, you often start breathing with short little breaths and your heart beats faster than usual. To make yourself feel calmer, you can S-L-O-W your breathing down by doing this...

START here and follow the blue shape with your finger as you breathe.

Take a deep breath IN through your NOSE ... S-L-O-W-L-Y

As you breathe IN, you could imagine that you can smell ...

a lovely flower,

a freshly baked pie,

or a special blanket.

And as you breathe slowly OUT, you could think about . . .

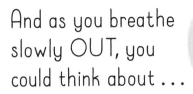

blowing on hot chocolate to cool it down,

blowing a huge bubble

or slowly blowing out some candles.

Breathe OUT through your mouth . . . VERY S-L-O-W-L-Y

Keep breathing IN and OUT and IN and OUT in this way until you feel calmer. You can do this wherever and whenever you feel worries or fears making you breathe too fast. Then it's time to . . .

Talk to someone

TALKING about your feelings is a really good way to stop worries from growing too big. First, you need to work out exactly what you are feeling and GIVE IT A NAME. Can you help these children name their feelings? (You can choose more than one for each child.)

I don't like it when Grandad's dog jumps up and barks. It makes me feel . . . .

They all know each other, but I'm new. I don't know what to say. I feel . . . .

If my mum is late picking me up from school, I feel . . . .

I don't want to jump into the water. I'm feeling too . . . .

I really want to go to Arlo's dinosaur party but I'm . . . . a balloon will pop.

SCARED   NERVOUS   LONELY   WORRIED

SHY   AFRAID   SAD

Talking about worries and fears can often help you find a way to feel better or even solve a problem. Sam (the child who's worried about balloons) has done some breathing and named some feelings. Now it's time to talk to someone about them. This is what Sam could say to Arlo:

SAM

> Arlo, I want to come to your party but I'm a bit WORRIED about it.

> I'm ... I'm ... really SCARED of balloons!

> Why are you worried, Sam? It's going to be fun!

> That's OK. It's a dinosaur party and dinosaurs don't like balloons. I'll tell my mum we don't need any.

ARLO

You can't ALWAYS just escape from worries like this, but TALKING to your friends and grown-ups can often help you find ways to do something about them. This is what Sam could say to Dad.

> Dad, you know I'm SCARED of balloons?

> Yes, Sam. I understand you don't feel safe around balloons.

> I'm really WORRIED that I'll never be able to go to parties.

> I have an idea for how we could help you. Shall we go to the park and have a chat about it? ★

And although we can't always get rid of ALL our worries and fears, there's a lot we CAN do to feel calmer and happy in our lives. Turn the page for some ideas.

★Grown-ups: See page 31 for ways that Dad could help Sam.

Get busy

If you get busy doing other things, you won't have so much time to worry. On the next few pages are some ideas for things you could do.

Humming and doodling makes me feel happy.

DUM DI DUM DI DUM DUM DUM

Do some doodling on a big piece of paper. Don't worry about what you doodle. Just enjoy doing it.

Colour in your doodles, or draw some patterns, then colour them in.

Draw your favourite animal or a pet. You could write its name and make up a poem or story about it.

Daisy the dolphin lives in the sea. She jumps and she dives with her friend named Dee.

Squish and squeeze some modelling clay with your hands. What can you turn it into?

Use some old pans, boxes or bins as drums and bash your worries away.

Line up your toys and tell them all about your day.

Getting busy won't make all your worries and fears disappear, but it can make you feel happier and gives you a break from thinking about them.

Make or do something

Making and doing things is another fantastic way of pushing worries out of your head. What could you make or do today?

Gather some recycling and stick things together to see what you can make.★

Make a book full of pictures of your family, friends and favourite places.

Make a den with a sheet and some chairs. Cuddle up inside with a blanket and a book.

Ask a grown-up to help you make something that everyone can eat.

★Make sure everything is clean before you start.

Doing something that you enjoy always helps when you begin to feel worried. Maybe you could . . .

Paint a picture?   Play an instrument?   Write a letter?   Or dress up?

Or why don't you . . .

build the highest tower you can with building blocks or cushions . . .

. . . then have fun knocking it down again?

When you find something that you really like doing, worries and fears don't seem so important. What fun things do YOU like to do?

Go outside

Being outdoors is a really good way to get away from your worries. It could be a garden, a park, or anywhere with trees and plants. (Don't forget to take a grown-up with you).

CHIRP CHIRP

If it's dry enough, lie on your back under a tree and spend a few moments just looking at the shapes that the leaves and branches make.

Now close your eyes ...
What can you **hear**?

BUZZZZZZZZZ

What can you **feel** under your hands?
Take a deep breath. What can you **smell**?

Take a close **look** at the ground. Are there any leaves, twigs, seeds or stones to collect?

Ooo! There's a little bug on this stone!

RUSTLE

You could use what you find to make a pattern on the ground.

Any time you feel worried, just look up at the sky. Are there any clouds drifting by?

What shapes can you see? Imagine your worries floating away with the clouds ...

Wherever you are outdoors, if you stay really still and really quiet for a while, you just might see an animal. What is it doing? How does it move?

Even just taking a walk in nature can help you feel calmer, so put on your shoes, grab your grown-up and go outside as often as you can.

Get moving!

When you get your body MOVING and stretching, it helps your brain let go of your worries. Doing some exercise is a lot of fun too.

S-T-R-E-T-C-H
your back down like a dog.

Balance on one leg like a flamingo.

MEOW!

S-T-R-E-T-C-H
your back up like a cat.

Try rolling like a ball.

HUFF PUFF

How fast can you run?

Reach for the sky!

S-T-R-E-T-C-H your hands up as high as you can.

Leap like a frog.

22

Skip with a rope.

Hello!

Or get out and about on a scooter.

Just dance!

Ha
ha
Hee
hee!

I CAN DO IT!

Can you touch your toes?
(Keep your legs straight!)

Bounce UP and DOWN like a little kangaroo.

How many jumps can you do?

...5
...6
...7
...8

Play a game of tag with your friends.
Who will be 'it' next?

Friends and family

Having fun with your friends and family is one of the very best ways to feel calm and happy. Here are some ideas for things to try.

Collect things around your home that are all the same colour. How many can you find?

One, two, three, four five ...

MEOW

Tell each other silly jokes.

Why did the banana go to the doctor?

We don't know!

HEE HEE!

It wasn't peeling well!

Play 'I spy with my little eye'.

Ha Ha

I spy with my little eye something beginning with B.

Basket?

No!

Balloon?

No!

BOTTOM?

YES!

Tap a balloon around to keep it in the air for as long as you can. Don't let it touch the ground!

Ha ha

Count the taps and try to beat your record.

Take turns to pretend to be an animal. Can your friend guess what you are?

SQUAWK!

FLAP

FLAP

CROAK, CROAK!

BOING

BOING

Draw five pictures of things that make YOU feel happy.

Sing together, and do some actions.

Row, row, row your boat, gently down the stream . . .

Watch something funny.

I LOVE this bit!

Ha ha

HEE

HEE

Play a board game or card game, or see if you can finish a jigsaw.

Your go!

What do YOU like to do with your family and friends?

Let them go . . .

Here are some ideas that might help you GET RID of your worries and fears, or at least stop them from bothering you so much.

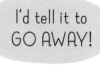

I'd tell it to GO AWAY!

I'd tell it to BE QUIET!

MEEP

MEEP

Imagine your worry as an annoying, noisy little creature. How could you get rid of it?

Scribble a picture of what your worry feels like. Then, scrunch it up and throw it in the bin.

Close your eyes and think of a happy place. Open your eyes and draw it.

Whenever you feel worried or scared, close your eyes, take some deep breaths and imagine your happy place.

If you are worried or nervous, try TALKING TO YOURSELF. You can do this out loud or in your head (and you can do this as often as you like).

I can do this!
I can do this!

It's OK.
It's OK.

Making a book about yourself can help you think about the good things in your life and stop worrying so much. Here's a page Sam has done.

My name is
Sam Sabuda

Things that I am good at

- ☑ Dancing
- ☑ Building towers
- ☑ Being kind
- ☑ Making pizza
- ☑ Singing

A picture of me

Three things that I like about myself

I can make elephant noises.

I am funny.

My hair

Things I can ALWAYS do if I begin to feel worried.

Breathe!
Ask for some help.
Sip some water.
Hug a toy.

Three things I enjoyed today

Pancakes

Playing dinosaurs with Arlo

PE with Miss Patel

Three things that are good in my life

Pizza on Fridays

My friends

Unicorn pyjamas

Three people I can talk to about my worries

Miss Patel, Auntie Flo, Dad

If you were making this book, what would you write or draw?

Helping each other

Did you know that being kind and helping our friends can actually make us feel good too? Choose the kindest thing to say if these children were your friends and they told you about a problem.

Lauryn tells you that she is worried because she has lost her bag.

Say, 'It's not MY problem!'

Say, 'Shall I help you look for it?'

Say, 'You're silly to lose your bag.'

Albie tells you that he is worried about going to dance club for the first time.

Say, 'Come with me and I'll show you what to do.'

Say, 'The dances are really hard to learn.'

Say, 'Don't be such a baby, Albie!'

Nisha says she is worried because her grandma isn't very well.

Say, 'That's YOUR problem, Nisha!'

Say, 'Well, I was ill last year.'

Say, 'Shall we make her a 'Get Well' card?'

Olivia says she is scared to go to big school because she can't read yet.

Say, 'Don't worry. You'll learn to read at school.'

Say, 'I don't care about that!'

Say, 'I can read. Why can't you?'

Ari says he is scared because he keeps forgetting the words of a song for a show.

Say, 'Well, everyone else knows the words.'

Say, 'Go away, Ari. It's not my problem!'

Say, 'We could sing it together until you know the words.'

Some notes for grown-ups

This book is designed to help young children recognize, understand and begin to learn to manage their anxieties. It is quite normal and even healthy to feel some fear and anxiety as it can help prepare us for potentially dangerous situations, adapt to meet challenges and sharpen our minds to perform well in exams and other stressful situations. But everyone needs to be aware of when anxiety and stress levels stop being 'normal' and start to become a problem. This is when they become so overwhelming, they stop us from doing things we usually enjoy, stop us from feeling happy and begin to have an impact on our lives and overall wellbeing.

Some common worries and fears in early childhood are:

- Loud or unexpected noises (especially for toddlers)
- Separation from parents or carers
- Monsters and the dark (especially for the 4 to 6 age-group)
- Scary dreams
- Bugs and creepy-crawlies
- Dogs or other big animals
- Social situations (extreme shyness)
- New experiences

How do I know if my child is anxious?

In very young children, anxiety may result in behavioural changes – they may become extremely clingy, tearful, withdrawn or angry. You may notice a deterioration in sleeping and eating patterns; reports of tummy aches, headaches and bad dreams, and bed-wetting in children who are usually dry at night. You may also notice an increase in 'controlling behaviours' such as becoming upset, distressed or angry at not having a choice over what they eat, at hearing the word "no", or when being told that it's bedtime. In extreme cases, they may develop nervous behaviour such as skin-picking or pulling out their hair.

How can I help?

We can't (and actually shouldn't) try to remove all sources of worry and fear from our children's lives because without them they don't get the opportunity to learn to manage risks and challenges and to develop RESILIENCE. This is the ability to endure and bounce back after times of adversity, disappointment, failure, a distressing event, and so on. What we CAN do is teach children how to recognize and manage their worries and fears so they don't become overwhelmed by them.

For the under seven age-group, 'talking' techniques are usually less effective than 'distraction activities' such as exercise, playing games and doing art projects, along with 'mindful' breathing and relaxation. This is why so much of this book concentrates on helping children learn to calm themselves in these ways. Even though 'doing' tends to work best, it's still a good idea to help young children recognize and identify their feelings. Being able to put worries into words is an important developmental skill and children who don't learn to process and manage feelings well can get 'stuck' emotionally and may find it hard to deal with everyday challenges.

20 ways to help children learn to manage their anxieties

1. Help them to understand that difficult feelings are part of everyday life, that there are ways to manage them and that they will pass.

2. Don't avoid all situations that they find stressful. (Avoidance can make anxiety worse.)

3. Don't always rush in to try to fix or solve whatever is upsetting your child (unless a situation is actually dangerous, of course).

4. Teach them how to think of possible solutions to problems and ways to manage their feelings. Listen and ask questions to help them come up with their own solutions.

5. Help them learn the vocabulary to name and talk about their feelings, and let them know that they can always ask for help if they feel anxious.

6. Let them hear you talking about your own feelings and strategies for managing and solving problems.

7. Practise the breathing technique shown on pages 12 and 13 with them, so that they learn how to slow down their breathing and heartbeat when they are feeling anxious.

8. Role-play meeting and greeting with toys to help children develop social skills — especially those who have social anxiety.

9. Encourage outdoor play and, if you can, provide the resources such as games, jigsaws, crayons and paper for the activities described in this book.

10. Help them make a 'worry box' from a shoe box with a slot cut into the top. They can post pictures, doodles and writing about their worries into the box to help them let go of them.

11. Buy or make some 'worry dolls' - tiny dolls inside a small bag. Your child tells their worries to the dolls, then puts them back in the bag one by one.

12. For children who are constantly expressing worried thoughts, you could try instigating 'worry time' - a period of 15 minutes a day when they can talk about their worries. Explain that the rest of the time they don't need to think about them.

13. Prepare your child before a big or new event, such as a house move or hospital appointment. Let them know what's likely to happen and why.

14. Try to stick to regular and soothing routines, especially around bedtime. Read or sing and let children know they are safe and loved.

15. Read all kinds of stories, not only happy ones. Talking about emotions in books is a good way to learn to understand them and to build empathy (the ability to imagine how others are feeling).

16. Books can also be useful to help older children talk about big things that may be upsetting them, such as bereavement, separation or illness.

17. Encourage children to think about and be grateful for the everyday good things in their lives, and think about positives: What are they good at? What do they like about themselves?

18. Help them make a 'Book About Me', like the one shown on page 27 to help build their self-esteem.

19. Help them understand mistakes aren't failures but the way that we learn and get better at things.

20. Monitor what they watch so that they are not exposed to inappropriate scary images on screens.

When your child is afraid

Much as you may feel like saying, "Don't be silly, there's nothing to be scared of!", it's important not to dismiss or trivialize children's fears, which to them are very real. It's better to validate their feelings to show that you understand (as Sam's dad does on page 15) and work out a plan for managing the fear together, such as the step-by-step one described below.

- Don't try to talk them out of being afraid, but acknowledge their feeling.

- Comfort them and hug them and let them know they are safe.

- Stay calm and confident when you talk to them.

- Practise coping responses – drawing, role-playing, playing with toys, breathing, etc.

- Don't force them to do more than they are comfortable with, but don't give them a total 'get out'. (Avoidance won't solve the problem.)

- Be patient – it takes time to overcome powerful feelings.

- Remember to praise your child's hard work to overcome their fear, and reward all efforts – big or small.

A step-by-step approach to managing a specific fear

For a specific fear, such as the one shown in this book (fear of balloons), a very gradual, gentle approach with plenty of encouragement, praise and rewards can work, for example:

1. Start off seeing if your child can touch an uninflated balloon a few times.
2. Next time, see if they can hold and play with an uninflated balloon.
3. Now, can they be in the same room while you blow a balloon up?
4. Then, see if they can touch the inflated balloon.
5. Now, can they hold and play with the inflated balloon?
6. Finally, and with plenty of warning and reassurance, see if they can be in the room where a balloon is deliberately popped.

At all times during this process (which may take weeks or months), it is important to reassure your child, keep them talking about how they are feeling, remind them that they are safe and that nothing bad is going to happen, repeat steps if necessary, and reward all their efforts. It may be that they never learn to like balloons (or dogs, or the dark, or whatever they are afraid of) but they may be able to develop enough coping strategies to be in the same room or area as them and not prevented from sleeping or doing the things they enjoy.

When to seek professional help

In time, most children grow out of their anxieties but, in the meantime, try some of the activities described in this book and offer them the help and reassurance they need, with plenty of hugs when they feel anxious. However, if you feel your child's anxiety is starting to affect their everyday life, it's a good idea to talk to your GP or Health Visitor, especially if your child's anxiety:

- severely restricts what they are able or willing to do
- has a marked impact on their usual routine or family life
- makes them reluctant to go to school, nursery or playgroup for a long period of time
- significantly disrupts their sleeping and eating patterns
- is accompanied by nervous habits such as skin-picking or hair-pulling
- includes severe phobias (irrational fears) of particular activities or objects

The treatment offered by most mental health professionals for anxiety disorders is known as cognitive behavioural therapy (CBT). CBT can help children as young as 5 to identify their anxiety and learn skills to reduce it. Parents may also be offered support to help manage their child's anxiety.

Be a good role-model

There is plenty you can do to help children manage their anxieties, but it's always worth thinking about whether they are picking up on your own: anxiety does tend to run in families and fears can be learnt. Anxiety is a treatable condition, and if you think you may need help, contact your GP who will be able to recommend treatment. There are also links to helpful websites at Usborne Quicklinks.

Usborne Quicklinks

Visit Usborne Quicklinks for links to carefully selected websites with activities that can help children cope with worries and fears, and video clips to share with them. There are also links to websites with helpful tips and advice for grown-ups too.

Go to usborne.com/Quicklinks and type in the keywords 'all about worries'. Children should be supervised online. Please read our internet safety guidelines at Usborne Quicklinks.